Dinosaurs

Steve Parker
Consultant: Dr Jim Flegg

miles Kelly

PUBLISHING

First published in 2002 by
Miles Kelly Publishing Ltd
Bardfield Centre, Great Bardfield, Essex, CM7 4SL

Copyright © Miles Kelly Publishing 2002
2 4 6 8 10 9 7 5 3 1

Some material in this book can also be found in *100 Things You Should Know About Dinosaurs.*

Editor: Amanda Learmonth

Design: Debbie Meekcoms

Assistant Editor: Nicola Sail

Index: Lynn Bresler

British Library Cataloguing-in-Publication Data
A catalogue record for this book is available from the British Library

ISBN 1-84236-110-4

Printed in Hong Kong

www.mileskelly.net
info@mileskelly.net

ACKNOWLEDGEMENTS

The Publishers would like to thank the following artists who have contributed to this book:

Chris Buzer (Studio Galante), Jim Channell (Bernard Thornton Illustration), Fiammetta Dogi (Scientific Illust.), Chris Forsey, Mike Foster (Maltings Partnership), L.R. Galante (Studio Galante), Brooks Hagan (Studio Galante), Alan Hancocks, Stuart Lafford (Linden Artists Ltd), Kevin Maddison, Alan Male (Linden Artists), Janos Marffy, Alessandro Menchi (Studio Galante), Massimiliano Maugeri (Studio Galante), Francesco Spadoni (Studio Galante), Rudi Vizi, Steve Weston (Linden Artists), Mike White (Temple Rogers)

Computer-generated artwork by James Evans

Contents

The dinosaur world

Dinosaurs were types of animals with scaly skin, called reptiles. They lived millions of years ago. There were many different kinds of dinosaurs, but they all died out long, long ago.

Corythosaurus *had a duck-like beak to scoop up plants.*

Tyrannosaurus *was a fierce meat-eater with powerful jaws.*

Triceratops *means 'three-horned face'.*

5

When were they around?

PALAEOZOIC ERA	MESOZOIC ERA	
PERMIAN PERIOD	TRIASSIC PERIOD	JURASSIC PERIOD

248 million years ago

The first proper dinosaurs appear. These are small, two-legged carnivores (meat-eaters) and larger herbivores (plant-eaters).

Erythrosuchus

Thrinaxodon

286 million years ago

The reptiles are becoming more important than the amphibians.

Riojasaurus

Plateosaurus

Barosaurus

Apatosaurus

Heterodontosaurus

208 million years ago

Many different dinosaurs lived at this time, including the giant plant-eaters like Barosaurus.

Dinosaurs lived between about 230 million and 65 million years ago. This vast length of time is called the Mesozoic Era. Dinosaurs were around for about 80 times longer than people have been on Earth!

Dinosaurs

MESOZOIC ERA

CRETACEOUS PERIOD

144 million years ago

During the last part of the Age of Dinosaurs, both giant carnivores and armoured herbivores were alive.

Tarbosaurus

Tyrannosaurus rex

Deinonychus

Spinosaurus

CENOZOIC ERA

TERTIARY PERIOD

Thylacosmilus, *meat-eating mammal*

Brontotherium, *plant-eating mammal*

Nesodon, *plant-eating mammal*

65 million years ago

The dinosaurs have all died out. The mammals, that have been around since the Triassic Period, become the main land animals.

Stegosaurus *was around for more than 20 million years. It was one of the longest lasting dinosaurs.*

Compsognathus *was one of the smallest dinosaurs known.*

Desmond's fun facts!

The name 'dinosaur' means 'terrible lizard'. But dinosaurs weren't lizards, and not all dinosaurs were terrible either!

Life before dinosaurs

Dinosaurs were not the first animals on Earth. Many other kinds of creatures lived before them, including many other types of reptiles. Over millions of years, one of these groups of reptiles probably changed very slowly, or evolved, into the first dinosaurs.

▼ *Dimetrodon was a fierce reptile that looked like a dinosaur – but it wasn't. It lived 270 million years ago, before the time of the dinosaurs.*

▲ Ornithosuchus was an early thecodont. This was a carnivore (meat-eater) that walked on two legs, a cousin of the first dinosaurs.

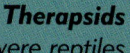

Erythrosuchus *was a crocodile that was around before the first dinosaurs.*

Therapsids *were reptiles with furry skin like mammals.*

Test your memory!

1. What type of animal was the dinosaur?

2. What is the name of the era in which dinosaurs lived?

3. Which dinosaur lasted for more than 200 million years?

4. Was Compsognathus one of the smallest or biggest dinosaurs known?

Plants *such as tree ferns existed at this time.*

1. a reptile 2. the Mesozoic Era 3. Stegosaurus 4. the smallest

9

Time for the dinosaurs

The earliest dinosaurs walked the Earth almost 230 million years ago. They lived in what is now Argentina, in South America. They included *Eoraptor* and *Herrerasaurus*. Both were slim and fast, and ran on their two back legs.

Herrerasaurus

Make a dinosaur move!

You will need:

- some stiff card
- safe scissors
- sticky tape • split pins

1. Cut out a model of Herrerasaurus. The head, body, arms and tail are one piece of card.

2. Cut out each leg from another piece. Fix the legs on either side of the hip area of the body using a split pin.

3. Move the angle of the head, body and tail to stand over the legs. This is how many dinosaurs moved, well balanced over their back legs.

Herrerasaurus *had legs under its body, unlike other reptiles.*

The head *was long, with a bendy neck to look round for prey.*

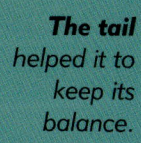

The tail *helped it to keep its balance.*

11

Changing dinosaurs

As the early dinosaurs spread over the land, they began to change. This natural change in living things has happened since life began on Earth. New kinds of plants and animals appear, do well for a time, and then die out as yet more new kinds appear. This slow change of living things over time is called evolution.

Plateosaurus

▶ *Some kinds of dinosaur became larger and began to eat plants rather than animals.*

Riojasaurus

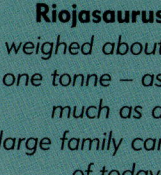

Riojasaurus
*weighed about
one tonne – as
much as a
large family car
of today.*

Plateosaurus
*was one of
the first big
plant-eating
dinosaurs.*

▼ Rutiodon was a
crocodile-like meat-eater

Desmond's fun facts!

*Early plant-eating
dinosaurs did
not eat fruits or
grasses – these
hadn't appeared
yet! Instead they
ate plants such
as horsetails
and ferns.*

Gentle giants

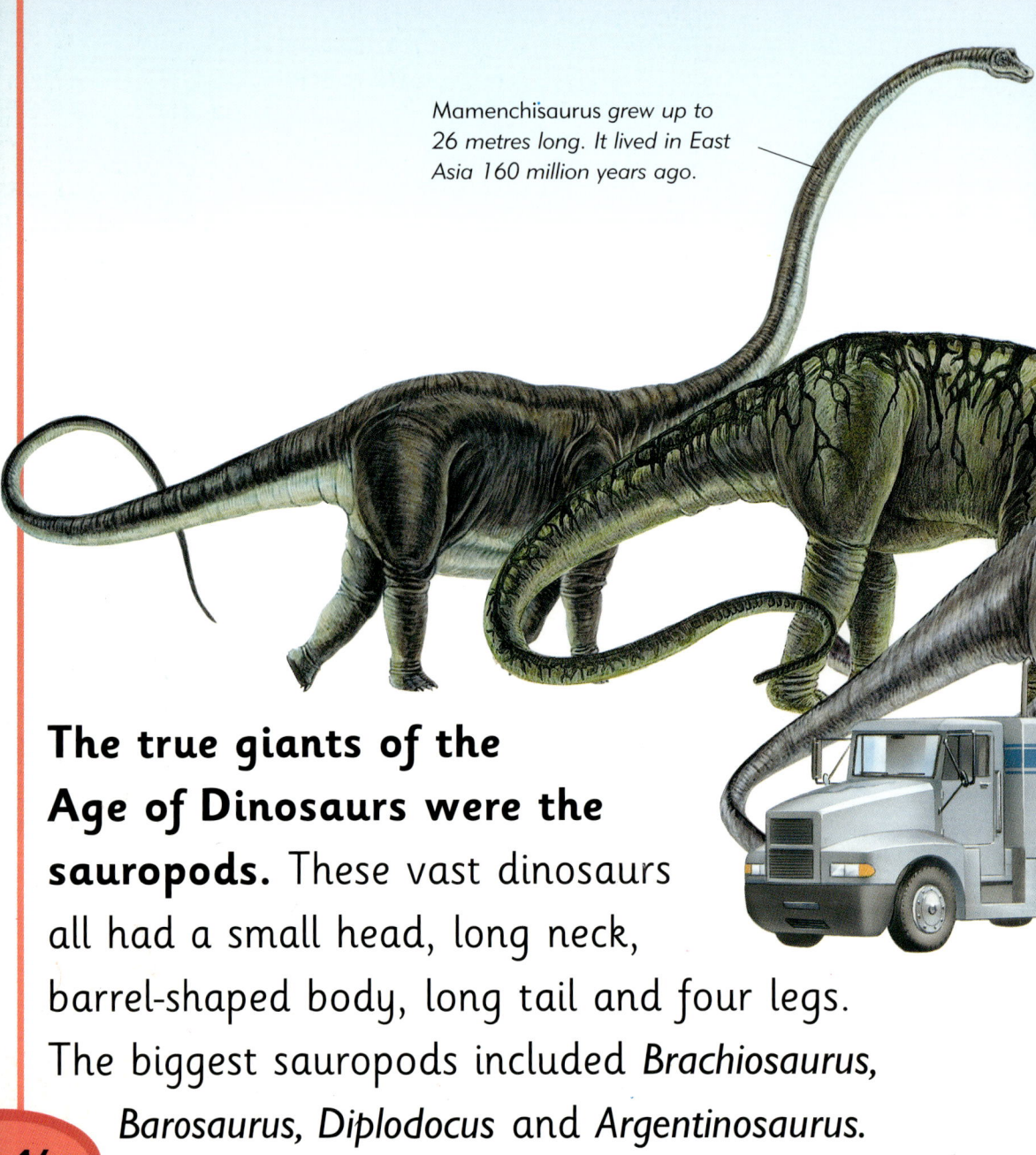

Mamenchisaurus *grew up to 26 metres long. It lived in East Asia 160 million years ago.*

The true giants of the Age of Dinosaurs were the sauropods. These vast dinosaurs all had a small head, long neck, barrel-shaped body, long tail and four legs. The biggest sauropods included *Brachiosaurus, Barosaurus, Diplodocus* and *Argentinosaurus*.

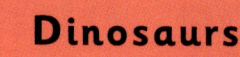

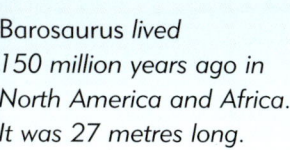

Barosaurus *lived 150 million years ago in North America and Africa. It was 27 metres long.*

Brachiosaurus *grew up to 25 metres long. It lived 150 million years ago in North America and Africa.*

Argentinosaurus *was the biggest sauropod – 40 metres long.*

Diplodocus *lived in North America 150 million years ago. It grew to 27 metres long.*

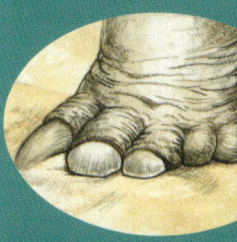

Sauropods *had flat claws which looked like toenails!*

This modern truck is to the same scale as these huge dinosaurs!

Desmond's fun facts!

Diplodocus *is also known as 'Old Whiptail'! It could swish its long tail so hard and fast that it made an enormous* CRACK *like a whip.*

Huge hunters

The biggest meat-eating dinosaurs were the largest predators (hunters) ever to have lived. Different types came and went during the Age of Dinosaurs. One of the last dinosaurs was also one of the largest – *Tyrannosaurus*.

◀ *Tyrannosaurus had sharp teeth and powerful jaws.*

Gigantosaurus *was the biggest carnivore (meat-eater).*

Allosaurus *had long, strong back legs for fast running.*

Desmond's fun facts!

Some meat-eating dinosaurs not only bit their prey, but also each other! Fossils of several Tyrannosaurus had bite marks on the head.

See, hear, smell

Like the reptiles of today, dinosaurs could see, hear and smell the world around them. We know this from fossils. Fossil skulls have spaces for eyes, ears and nostrils.

▲ Troodons *had very big eyes, which may have helped them to see in the dark.*

Make a Troodon *mask!*

You will need: card • safe scissors • elastic band

1. Ask an adult to help. Carefully cut out the shape below. Cut out two small eye holes.

2. Attach elastic to put the mask on. Look at how little you can see.

3. Carefully make the eye holes as large as the eyes of the real Troodon. Now you can have a much bigger, clearer view of the world!

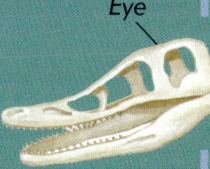

Eye

Troodon's *skull* shows large holes for the eyes.

Crest

Parasaurolophus may have used its tube-like crest to make a noise like a trumpet.

Corythosaurus had a bony plate on its head, instead of a tube.

Living with dinosaurs

All dinosaurs walked and ran on land, as far as we know. No dinosaurs could fly in the air or live in the water. But many other creatures, which lived at the same time as the dinosaurs, could fly or swim. Some were reptiles, like the dinosaurs.

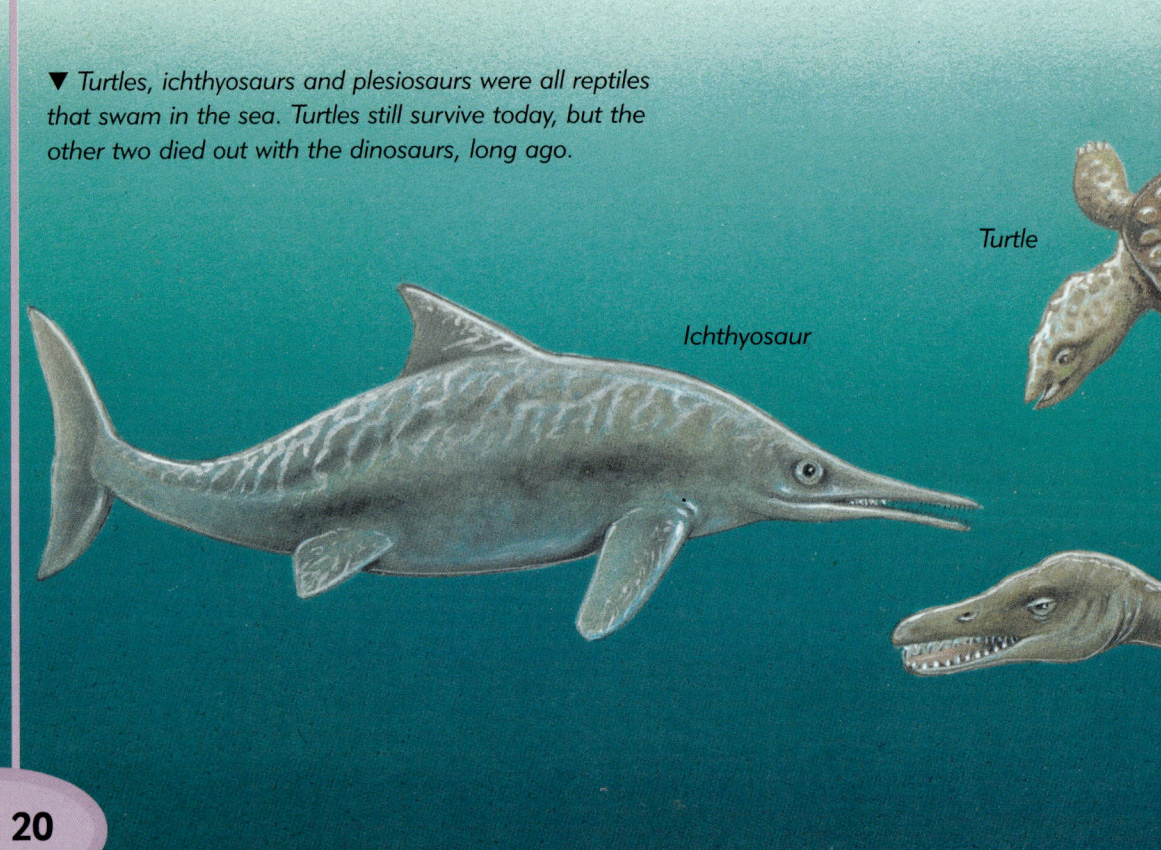

▼ *Turtles, ichthyosaurs and plesiosaurs were all reptiles that swam in the sea. Turtles still survive today, but the other two died out with the dinosaurs, long ago.*

Turtle

Ichthyosaur

Dinosaur quiz

Which of these are NOT dinosaurs?

A. Raptor **B.** Plesiosaur **C.** Hadrosaur

D. Ichthyosaur **E.** Bird

B. Plesiosaur D. Ichthyosaur E. Bird

Velociraptor could have grown feathers and slowly evolved into the first birds.

Ichthyornis was a bird that lived at the same time as the dinosaurs.

Plesiosaur

Rhamphorhynchus was a reptile that could fly.

21

Slow or speedy?

Dinosaurs walked and ran at different speeds, depending on their size and shape. In the world today, cheetahs and ostriches are slim with long legs and run very fast. Elephants and hippos are heavy and walk slowly. Dinosaurs were similar. Some were big, heavy and slow. Others were slim, light and speedy.

Speedy quiz

Put these dinosaurs and today's animals in order of top running speed, from slowest to fastest.

Human (40 km/h)   Cheetah (100-plus km/h)   Struthiomimus (70 km/h)

Muttaburrasaurus (15 km/h)   Sloth (0.2 km/h)   Coelophysis (30 km/h)

Sloth, Muttaburrasaurus, Coelophysis, Human, Struthiomimus, Cheetah

Struthiomimus *was one of the fastest of all dinosaurs.*

▼ Coelophysis was a slim dinosaur that could probably run around very quickly.

Early dinosaurs walked on all four legs, and could not move very quickly.

Muttaburrasaurus *could only run around 15 km per hour.*

23

Dinosaurs in battle

Some dinosaurs had body defences against predators. These might be large horns and spikes, or hard lumps of bone like armour-plating. Most armoured dinosaurs were plant-eaters. They had to defend themselves against big meat-eating dinosaurs such as *Tyrannosaurus.*

Styracosaurus

Euoplocephalus

Protoceratops

Design a dinosaur

Make an imaginary dinosaur! It might have the body armour and tail club of Euoplocephalus, or the horns and neck frill of Triceratops.

You can draw your dinosaur, make it out of pieces of card or from modelling clay. You can give it a made-up name, like 'Euoplo-ceratops' or 'Tri-cephalus'.

How well protected is your dinosaur? Is it anything like creatures of today?

Euoplocephalus used the hard lump on its tail as a club for hitting enemies.

Triceratops

Triceratops had three horns for charging at predators.

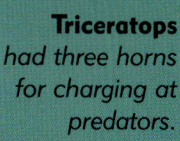

Protoceratops may have used its neck frill to frighten off its enemies.

Eggs and nests

Like most reptiles today, dinosaurs produced young by laying eggs. These hatched out into baby dinosaurs which gradually grew into adults. Fossils have been found of eggs with dinosaurs still developing inside, as well as fossils of just-hatched baby dinosaurs.

▶ *A female* Protoceratops *scraped a bowl-shaped nest across the dry soil.*

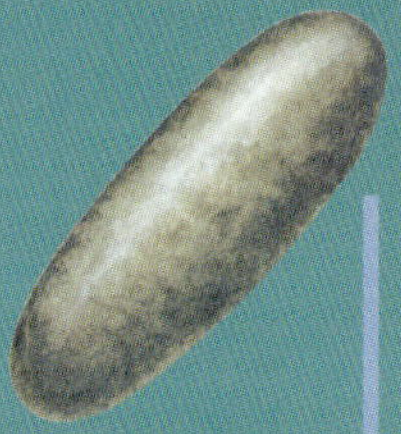

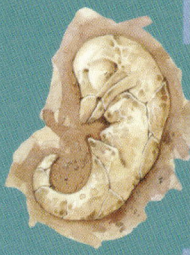

Protoceratops' eggs were placed in circles inside the nest.

A fossilized baby developing inside an egg.

The hadrosaur egg was leathery and bendy, like reptile eggshells of today.

Test your memory!

1. How many horns did Triceratops have?

2. Was Struthiomimus one of the fastest or slowest dinosaurs?

3. Out of the turtle, the ichthyosaur and the plesiosaur, which reptile is still around today?

1. three 2. fastest 3. the turtle

Baby dinosaurs

Some dinosaur parents looked after their babies and even brought them food in the nest. Fossils of the hadrosaur dinosaur *Maiasaura*, shown below, included nests, eggs, babies after hatching, and broken eggshells.

◀ The newly hatched Maiasaura babies had to stay in the nest. They could not run away as their legs were not strong enough.

A baby Maiasaura was only 30 to 40 centimetres long.

Berries were fed to the babies in their nests.

Desmond's fun facts!

Baby dinosaurs grew up to five times faster than human babies. Some were already one metre long when they hatched!

Where did they all go?

All dinosaurs on Earth died out by 65 million years ago. There are dinosaur fossils in the rocks up to this time, but there are none after. There are, though, fossils of other creatures like fish and mammals. What happened to wipe out some of the biggest animals that ever lived? There are many ideas. It could have been one, or many, disasters.

▼ *The dinosaurs may have been killed by a giant lump of rock, called a meteorite.*

Meteorite smash!

You will need:
- a plastic bowl • cooking flour • a large pebble
- a desk light • a place where mess does not matter!

1. Ask an adult to help. Put the flour in the bowl. This is Earth's surface.
2. Place the desk light so it shines over the bowl. This is the Sun. The pebble is the meteorite from space.
3. WHAM! Drop the pebble into the bowl. See how the tiny bits of flour float in the air like a mist, making the 'Sun' dimmer. A real meteorite smash may have been the beginning of the end for the dinosaurs.

Volcanoes could have erupted and choked the dinosaurs to death.

Plagues of animals could have eaten all the dinosaurs' eggs.

A giant tidal wave could have drowned the dinosaurs.

31

What came next?

From 65 million years ago there were no dinosaurs left. Dinosaurs were not the only group of animals to die out at that time. Some of the flying reptiles and swimming reptiles also died. When a group of living things dies out completely, this is known as extinction.

Desmond's fun facts!

No one really knows why some reptiles survived but the dinosaurs didn't – it still puzzles dinosaur experts to this day!

▼ *After the extinction of the dinosaurs, insects, worms, fish, birds and mammals all survived. These groups, shown here, are still alive today.*

Hesperocyon
was a mammal that was similar to rats of today.

Diatryma
was a giant bird that could not fly.

Hyracotherium
was an early horse with toes, not hooves.

33

What they left behind

We know about dinosaurs mainly from their fossils. Fossils took millions of years to form. Most fossils form on the bottoms of rivers or seas, where sand and mud can quickly cover them over and begin to preserve (keep) them.

Fossils take millions of years to form. Firstly, an animal, like this trilobite, dies. Trilobites lived in the sea about 600 million years ago, long before the first dinosaurs.

The soft parts rot away.

Fossil quiz

What formed fossils?
Which body parts of a dinosaur were most likely to become fossils?
Remember, fossils form from the hardest bits that last long enough to become buried in the rocks and turned to stone.

skull bone   muscle   leg bone   scaly skin   blood   claws   eye   teeth

skull bone, leg bone, teeth and claws are most likely to form fossils

Dinosaurs

The remaining shell is buried in mud.

The mud turns to rock, which turns the shell to rock, and makes a fossil.

A Tyrannosaurus skull shows its deadly, sharp teeth.

Dinosaur footprints became buried in the ground and turned into fossils.

A dinosaur skin fossil shows us how it was scaly, like reptile skin.

▲ The skull of Stegoceras was dome-shaped and thick. From this, scientists have guessed that they may have had head-butting contests.

35

Finding fossils

Every year, thousands of dinosaur fossils are discovered. From the fossils, scientists try to work out what the dinosaur looked like and how it lived, all those millions of years ago.

▼ These are palaeontologists, scientists that look for and study dinosaur bones.

Test your memory!

1. What is the big lump of rock that could have fallen on the dinosaurs?

2. What is it called when a group of animals dies out completely?

3. Where do most fossils form – on the land or in rivers and seas?

1. a meteorite 2. extinction 3. in rivers and seas

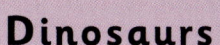

People dig into the rock with hammers and brushes.

Scientists make notes and sketches to record what they find.

Fossils are carefully lifted to stop them cracking.

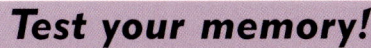

37

New fossil finds

The first fossils of dinosaurs to be studied by scientists came from Europe and North America. However, since those early discoveries in the 1830s and 1840s, dinosaur fossils have been found all over the world.

▶ Jobaria *and* Janenscia *are two giant sauropods from Africa that have been discovered recently.*

Desmond's fun facts!

One dinosaur is named after a young girl. Leaellynasaura was named after the daughter of the scientists who found its fossils!

▼ *Some of the most exciting fossils are being found in China. Many more are being discovered in Australia, Africa and South America.*

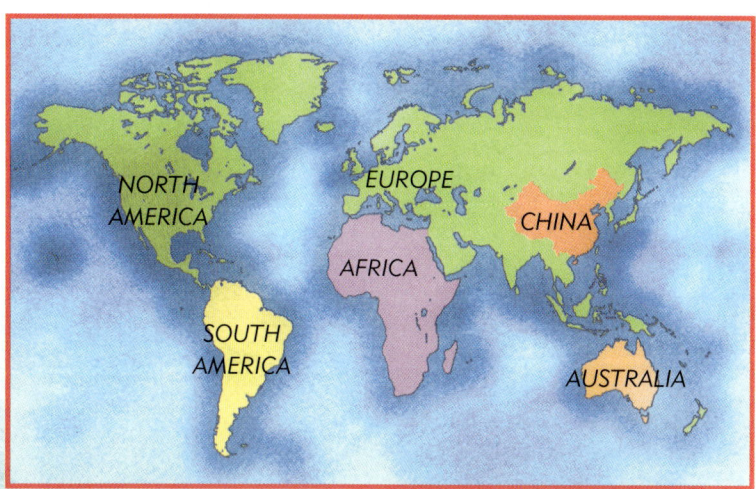

NORTH AMERICA

EUROPE

CHINA

AFRICA

SOUTH AMERICA

AUSTRALIA

Sinosauropteryx *was a bird-like creature. Its fossils were found in China.*

Caudipteryx *may have had feathers, so was it a bird or a dinosaur?*

Leaellynasaura *was discovered in 1989 in Australia.*

39

Index